Coloring **ART**

MW00568024

Illustrated by Amanda Murphy

Modern Elegance
COLORING BOOK

45+ Romantic Designs to
Color for Fun & Relaxation

Claire *Claire* *Clo* *Clair-* *r* *C* *Clo* *Claire*

Photo courtesy of BERNINA of America Inc.

Meet the Artist

Always attracted to color, texture, and pattern, Amanda Murphy has been designing, drawing, and sewing since she was a child. After graduating with a bachelor of fine arts degree from Carnegie Mellon University, she worked as a graphic designer and art director in Alexandria, Virginia, and New York City.

Amanda discovered quilting, an art that marries her passion for design with her enthusiasm for handwork. She markets her own full-color quilt pattern line under the Amanda Murphy Design label and has designed several fabric collections including Carina, her first line for Benartex. Amanda is also a BERNINA quilting and longarm spokesperson.

She is the author of *Modern Holiday; Color Essentials—Crisp & Vibrant Quilts; Free-Motion Quilting Idea Book;* and *Quilted Celebrations.*

Amanda lives in North Carolina with her family.
Learn more about Amanda at amandamurphydesign.com.

C&T PUBLISHING ctpub.com   P.O. Box 1456 • Lafayette, CA 94549 • 800.284.1114   Copyright ©2015 by Amanda Murphy. All rights reserved.

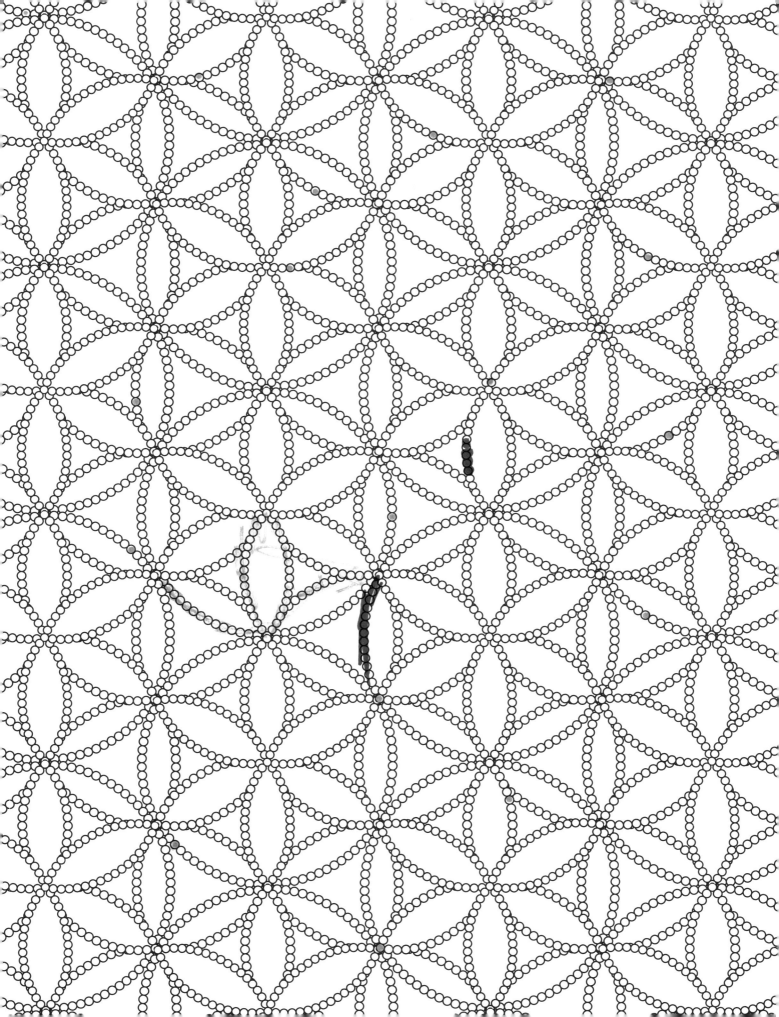

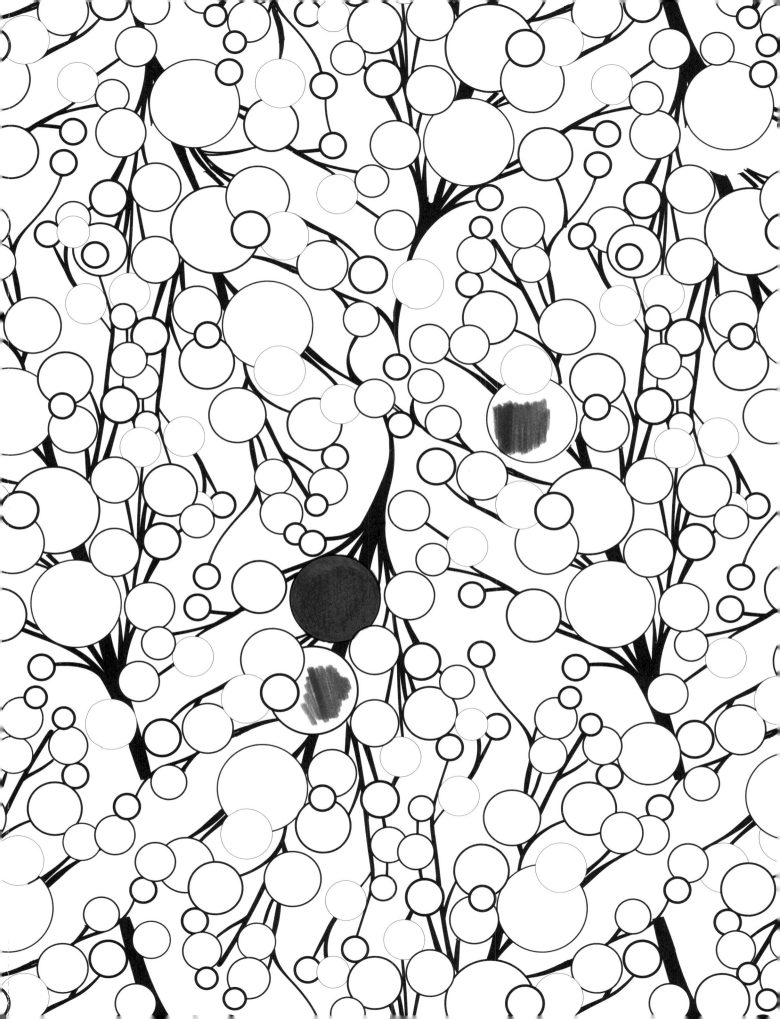

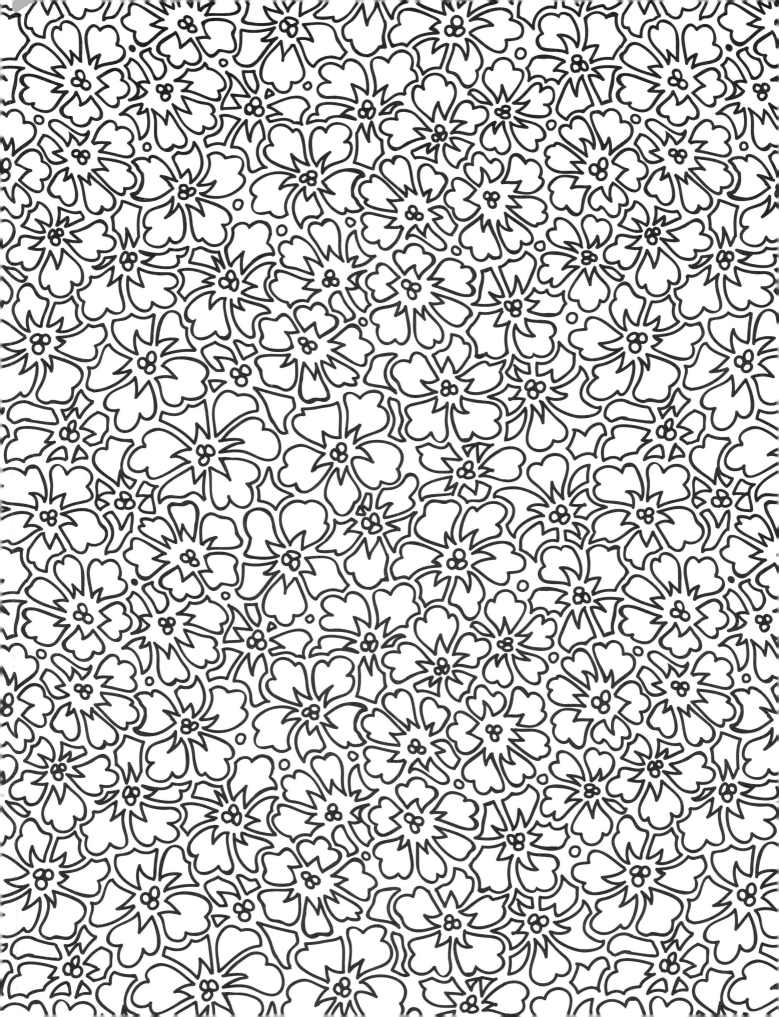

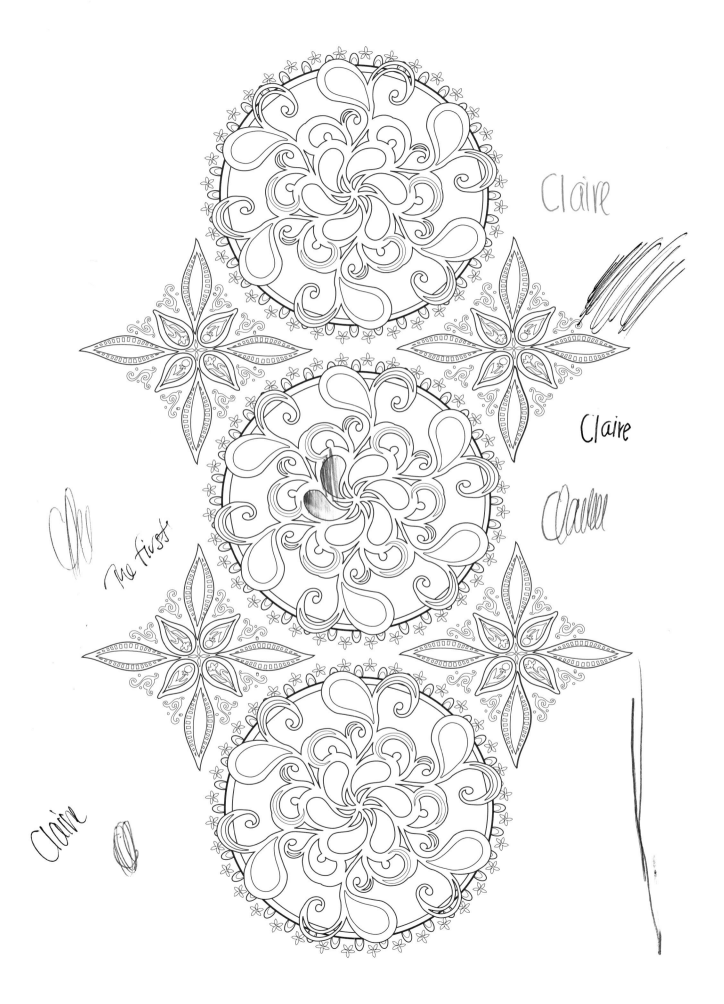

Claire

Claire

The first

Claire